Wildflowers in the Cracks

A daisy pops out, wearing shades of green,
In the sidewalk's grip, it's a sight to be seen.
It shimmies and shakes, saying, 'Look at me!'
In a world full of concrete, it's wild and free.

Cracks in the pavement sing out at night,
As dandelions wiggle, basking in starlight.
They throw a party while cars zoom on by,
Who knew that weeds could touch the sky?

Echoes of Regeneration

Out in the garden, the worms have a feast,
Turning trash into treasure, nature's grand beast.
They giggle and wiggle with quite a fine flair,
Making soil where once it was barren and bare.

The sun winks down, rays warm as can be,
A flower shouts, 'Hey! Come take a look at me!'
Bees buzz in chorus, a humorous choir,
While plants trade puns, their spirits on fire.

The Whispering Soil

The ground below chuckles, soft as a lull,
Promising blooms while it gives a gentle pull.
'Take a chance, dear seed, dive right in there!
Trust the whispers that tickle the air.'

With each playful burrow, a sprout shoots up,
Filling the world with laughter, like a cheer-filled cup.
Soil's happy jokes grow tall, making the matches,
Comedy gold beneath all the patches.

Renewal in the Stillness

In a garden where weeds held a dance,
Tomatoes joked, 'We'll take a chance!'
Sunflowers giggled, reaching for the sky,
While lazy ants just strolled by.

A worm in pajamas was digging a hole,
'Just cleaning my room!' was his funny goal.
The daisies chuckled at the earth's great tease,
As the morning dew gave everyone a freeze.

Original title:
Roots of Renewal

Copyright © 2025 Creative Arts Management OÜ
All rights reserved.

Author: Beckett Sinclair
ISBN HARDBACK: 978-1-80567-004-9
ISBN PAPERBACK: 978-1-80567-084-1

Awakening from the Past

In the attic, dust bunnies dance,
Old shoes hold their breath, taking a chance.
Mothballs giggle behind closed doors,
As Grandma's stories jump on the floors.

Casseroles bubble, ancient and bold,
Each one telling secrets, never told.
With a wink and a chuckle, they come alive,
Telling the tales of the past to thrive.

Channels of Change

A squirrel devised a new nutty plan,
'Let's change our diet to a peanut gran!'
The trees just laughed, shaking their leaves,
'Change is best served with some jolly jokes, please.'

The river swirled, wearing a goofy grin,
'I'm not flowing south, just practicing my spin!'
Fish caught the laughter from currents so wild,
While frogs croaked along, feeling like a child.

The Promise of New Canopies

A little seed dreamed of being a tree,
'With branches so wide, I'll feel so free!'
But first, it faced a tall stack of rocks,
Cried, 'If I trip, I'll wear funny socks!'

The clouds overhead whispered secrets of rain,
'Let's sprinkle and giggle, there's no need for pain!'
As the sunbeams radiated their sparkly cheer,
The saplings danced, 'We're blessed to be here!'

Nature's Embrace of Tomorrow

A flower opened its petals with flair,
'Watch me bloom, do you see me dare?'
Bees buzzing nearby joined the sweet fun,
'Let's make next year's honey a sticky pun!'

The breeze tickled leaves as they swung to and fro,
'What a wild ride, let's put on a show!'
The hilltops chuckled, echoing the joy,
As nature danced, a blissful ploy.

Flourish from the Fracture

In a garden where chaos reigns,
A flower sneezes, breaks the chains.
It stretches high, in search of sun,
Cackling loudly, 'Life's just begun!'

Cracks in concrete, oh what a sight,
Dandelions dancing, what a delight!
Pavement's no match for a seed's wild cheer,
'With a little sunlight, I'll disappear!'

The Pulse of Creation

A worm wiggled through a pile of glee,
'This dirt's the best, come party with me!'
Earthworms giggle, create a parade,
Who knew soil could have such a charade?

A sprout wobbled, unsure of the game,
'What's this, a dance? I'll stake my claim!'
With roots entwined like friends in a hug,
In the soil's rhythm, they all start to chug.

Birth of the Green

A tiny seed took a leap one day,
'Time to shine bright, I can't fade away!'
It popped through the soil with a laugh and grin,
'Leaf me alone, let the fun begin!'

The sun peeked in, a cheeky old chap,
'You're not going solo, now take a nap!'
But our brave sprout said, 'I'll always grow!'
'Just watch me dance, let the good times flow!'

Quiet Moments of Awakening

In a still corner, without a sound,
A sleepy sprout gets tangled around.
'This nap's so nice, but dreams can't be stalled,'
'Playtime awaits when the sun gets hauled!'

As the moon snickers, it pulls back the night,
Our sprout mumbles, 'I'll still reach for light!'
With giggles and yawns, the world starts to tease,
'Awake at last? Come dance in the breeze!'

The Song of Old Branches

Old branches creak and sway,
Like grannies in their chairs, they play.
With tales of youth, they laugh and shout,
While squirrels steal their nuts about.

They dance in wind, a kooky show,
A waltz with leaves that start to grow.
Each bark has wisdom, sweet as pie,
But still can't climb or even fly.

Rise from Ashes

A phoenix once said, "I'm a grill gone too far!"
"I'm just here chilling, no need for a scar."
With feathers of flame, it took quite a leap,
As marshmallows toasted, oh memories to keep!

Out of the ashes, I swear I can smell,
Sweet hot dogs roasting, can't you tell?
But without some ketchup, I surely can't thrive,
So pass me the buns! Let's get this party alive!"

Rebirth in the Garden

In the garden, where plants like to strut,
A daisy said, "Hey, stop stepping on my butt!"
They sprouted their flowers, wearing colors so bright,
While bees buzzed around, getting tipsy at night.

A tomato was blushing, had secrets to share,
"I've got a crush on that pumpkin over there!"
With laughter and blooms, they all planned a ball,
"Let's dance till we drop, or until we get small!"

New Beginnings in the Old

In the cluttered shed, old tools gather dust,
"Are we vintage or lost? It's a matter of trust."
A rusty old wrench piped up with a flare,
"I can fix a bike, if you just give me air!"

The garden hose laughed, "You might have some luck,
But without me, buddy, you're surely out of pluck!"
They cackled and giggled, 'til the sun started to set,
Sometimes old things just need a fresh mindset!"

Songs of the Resilient

In a garden of giggles, we find our cheer,
With daisies and dandelions, oh my dear!
A sprinkle of sunshine, a splash of rain,
Watch the silly blooms dance, driving us insane.

The worms wear top hats, the bugs sing tunes,
While rabbits do yoga beneath the full moons.
The bumblebee band plays a jazzy beat,
As flowers throw parties, can't stay off their feet!

So here's to the blossoms in wild, wacky regalia,
Each petal a jester, a colorful failure.
With smiles of petals, they grace the ground,
Life's a circus of joy, in laughter we're drowned.

Underneath this laughter, the fun we borrow,
The blooms just remind us, there's joy in tomorrow!

Budding Promises

In the corner, a plant does stare,
Wishing for sunlight, a little fresh air.
It stretches and yawns, so full of its dreams,
Thinking of veggies, not just leafy schemes.

A worm wiggled by, with a grin and a glee,
"Oh look at me dance! I'm as free as can be!"
The plant rolled its eyes, "You and your dirt!"
"At least I have roots, it's you that looks hurt!"

Where the Old Meets the New

In a crossover of young and old,
Lenors and millennials, both bold.
With ancient wisdom and modern flair,
They pull a prank, then stop and stare.

The old folks crack a joke or two,
While techies swipe and scroll right through.
Together they bloom, odd but true,
In this garden wild, a hullabaloo.

Gathering of the Blossoms

Blossoms chuckle in the breeze,
Wearing caps made out of leaves.
They plan a party just for fun,
With pollen cakes for everyone!

The bees are buzzing, disco balls,
While butterflies do silly sprawls.
Each hue a joke, a giggling hue,
As blossoms bloom, they bid adieu.

Echoes of Enlightenment

Echoes drift like puns from trees,
Philosophy in whispers, please!
They ponder life with roots entwined,
Yet couldn't remember what they find.

With laughter ringing through the glade,
They reminisce on past parades.
An oak will tell you he's quite wise,
But can't recall the reasons why!

Beneath the Weathered Bark

Oh, the squirrels hold meetings beneath the old trees,
Discussing acorns and long-forgotten keys.
The bark whispers secrets of tales from the past,
Of trees who grew funky and loved to have a blast.

Chipmunks wear shades, gazing up at the sky,
While branches swing low, giving high fives nearby.
Moss makes for pillows, it's cozy and neat,
Join the laughter parade on this woodland retreat.

The owls wear tuxedos, they're ready to dance,
In moonlit soirées, they give chance a chance.
Fungi are fashionistas, growing their best,
In the style of the forest, there's never a rest.

Under the weathered bark, the old and the spry,
Invite all the critters who want to just fly!

The Heartbeat of Renewal

In springtime's embrace, the giggles commence,
With flowers all blooming in vibrant suspense.
A daffodil wiggles, a tulip does twist,
Who knew that the soil could dance like this?

The sunbeams are tickling the leaves overhead,
While crickets do karaoke, their voices widespread.
Each bud has a secret, a pun to unveil,
In the laughter of nature, there's never a fail.

The bees in their jackets are buzzing away,
While ladybugs twirl in a spontaneous ballet.
Gently coaxing the sprouts, they hum a light tune,
Every chorus of green sings beneath the full moon.

Laughter is blooming in every bright patch,
As nature's own jesters continue to hatch!

Ferns and Fernweh

These ferns are all dreaming of places afar,
They chat about things like a fancy bazaar.
With fronds swaying lightly, and roots in a twist,
Their wanderlust tickles—it's too hard to resist!

"Let's leap to the tropics, wear flowers in hair!"
They giggle and wiggle, with a flair so rare.
Like adventurers lost in a soft green embrace,
Each frond is a traveler's whimsical grace.

With water and sun, ferns frolic and play,
They sip from the dew while the clouds float away.
"Let's visit the canopies, go show off our moves!
An expedition of fun, let's see how it grooves!"

Boundless their laughter, a true ferny parade,
With wiggles and jigs, none shall ever fade!

Fertile Ground

In a garden where weeds laugh loud,
A rabbit hops, feeling quite proud.
It digs for snacks, oh what a feast,
While gnawing on carrots, saying the least.

The sun shines bright on this silly scene,
As bugs do the jitterbug, like a queen.
The flowers all giggle, their petals a-flutter,
While seedlings play tag in the rich, warm butter.

Roots Beneath the Ice

Under the snow, a dance is in store,
Where sprouts and snowsprites have an uproar.
With no one to see, they giggle and slide,
In coats made of frost, they twirl with pride.

The trees are all chuckling, their branches a-sway,
While critters in burrows join in this play.
Icicles drip like a dripping wet joke,
As squirrels crack up, nearly go broke.

Life After the Fall

After the leaves take their tumble-bumble,
The critters all chat, not one single grumble.
With acorns in hand, they plan for a feast,
Reminiscing of summer, a nutty "at least!"

And in the crisp air, a joke makes the rounds,
As foxes in scarves prance on the grounds.
Fungi wear hats, and mushrooms do sing,
Of all the fun that the cold weather brings!

The Hidden Springs

Beneath the moss, there's a party quite cheeky,
With frogs in tuxedos feeling quite freaky.
They sip on the droplets, their fun never ends,
As fish join in, declaring them friends.

The water does twirl in a dance of delight,
While dragonflies buzz 'round, taking flight.
It's a giggle-filled gala, with all of the gang,
As nature's own symphony effortlessly sang.

Nurtured by the Earth

In the soil, the veggies laugh,
One carrot says, "I'm on the path!"
A potato rolls, a big old grin,
Says, "Let's dig deep and find some kin!"

The worms below throw quite the bash,
They wiggle and squirm, then make a splash!
While daisies dance under the sun's gaze,
Singing, "Come join our silly ways!"

Rebirth in the Canopy

High above, the branches sway,
With chattering birds in a fun ballet.
A squirrel jokes, with a nut in tow,
"I'm just planting seeds, don't feel the blow!"

The leaves gossip, rustling with glee,
"Who wore green best? Come on, let's see!"
They giggle and wiggle in the spring's show,
Pollinating bees say, "Let's start the glow!"

Whispers of the Undergrowth

Beneath the ferns, the critters croak,
A toad exclaims, "What a funny joke!"
Ants march in lines, a marching band,
Singing, "Follow us, let's make a stand!"

The mushrooms chuckle with a caps' flair,
"We're slimy and squishy, but we don't care!"
In this shady place, it's a hearty mix,
Nature's comedians pulling their tricks!

From Ashes to Abundance

Once were flames, now sprouting greens,
Wily weeds hide in their routines.
"What's this?" says a chard with a shine,
"I snuck through the ashes; now I'm divine!"

With laughter and cheer, they rise every day,
"Life's too short for a gloomy say!"
In their bountiful bloom, the plants convene,
In a fiesta of colors, bright and keen!

Renewed Horizons

In a garden, weeds take flight,
They dance around like mad at night.
A gopher plays the trombone loud,
While rabbits form a circus crowd.

The sun shines down with a goofy grin,
It tickles plants to make them spin.
The daisies giggle, swaying so bright,
And clouds join in for a cloudy fight.

New buds peek out, quite unafraid,
They stretch their arms, in sun they wade.
A ladybug wears shades of blue,
Strutting around like it's debut.

And off in the corner, seeds are glum,
They form a band, "We're the Underground!"
Yet in the wink of a playful breeze,
They grow up tall, do I hear cheese?

The Secrets Below

A worm with dreams of fame and cheer,
Writes a book, but can't find the gear.
He talks to radishes, wise and spry,
"Just wait," they say, "you'll soon be fly!"

The carrots scheme a grand ballet,
While onions practice hip-hop sway.
They form a clan, "The Veggie Crew,"
Polished roots with a raucous view.

A celery sticks to his daily grind,
"Join me or get left behind!"
But all the sprouts just roll their eyes,
As lettuce laughs with leafy sighs.

Under the ground, a party brews,
With wild beats and funky shoes.
When spring arrives, the news will spread,
The underground scene will be widespread!

From Silence to Symphony

In the quiet, mushrooms pop,
With little giggles, they just won't stop.
A toadstool plays on a tiny drum,
While crickets chirp, "Let's go dumb!"

The trees sway to the rhythm played,
Their branches moving like a parade.
A squirrel joins with a clumsy tap,
As nature sings a raucous rap.

A brook hums softly, setting the tone,
As leaf notes flutter, gently blown.
The flowers sway with powdery coats,
Bursting laughter in the throaty notes.

As night falls, stars join in the dance,
Making fireflies twinkle, take a chance.
The darkness giggles, shadows beam,
Symphony played on a moonbeam dream!

Flickers of Hope

An old boot sprouted a sprig of green,
Declared itself the queen, so keen!
It shouted, "Look, I have a purpose!"
While lost in thought—"Is it worth this?"

A chain of petals, wobbly and bright,
As the wind howled, filled with delight!
"Don't worry," sings a daisy in bloom,
"A little quirk adds fabulous room!"

Sunbeams shimmer with comical flair,
A beam of brightness in every layer.
The ground trembles from laughter so loud,
As weeds form a terribly proud crowd.

With each sprout, there's chatter and fun,
In the muck, new life has begun.
So here's to the oddball, the twist of fate,
A giggle sprouts from what we create!

Bridges to the Future

What will they think of our old ways,
When robots start dancing through our days?
Will they laugh at our vintage cars,
Or cherish our dreams held beneath the stars?

With every quirk and silly blunder,
We build new trails, sometimes with thunder.
Each step we took, each silly dance,
Leads to tomorrow, give change a chance!

Will they find joy in our memes made clear?
Or peek through a filter of digital cheer?
In giggles and laughter, we'll take a stand,
Creating a future that's quirky and grand!

So bring on the chaos, the jests and fun,
The future is bright; we're not yet done!
With bridges of humor, we'll leap and sway,
Together we'll navigate the new ballet!

Tapestry of Life

Threads of madness sewn with glee,
In this patchwork quilt, come sit with me.
Each square a blunder, each stitch a tale,
Together we laugh, we never pale.

With wild patterns and colors bright,
Our tapestry sparkles, a comical sight.
From cat memes to oddball jokes,
We weave in the laughter, our hearts it pokes.

Remember the time with a pie in the face?
We stitch it in laughter; there's no need for grace.
With each thread tangled, we find the way,
Through laughter and joy, we dance and play.

So share your quirks, your fun and your flair,
In this fabric of ours, there's always room to share.
A tapestry woven with giggles and cheer,
In this crazy work of art, we hold dear!

The Warmth Beneath

Beneath the surface, the giggles grow,
With jokes and jests, our spirits glow.
Like underneath earth where pumpkins hide,
We chuckle and snicker, our joy our guide.

Under hats too big or shoes too small,
We bounce through life, we bounce, we sprawl.
In the warmth of hugs that smell like pie,
We find our comfort, we laugh and sigh.

Frogs in tuxedos croak out a tune,
As fireflies twinkle beneath the moon.
With every chuckle that warms the night,
We dance 'round the flames, it feels so right.

So here's to the warmth, to jokes we share,
To the funny moments, our carefree air.
Beneath the surface, we may just find,
A treasure trove of silliness intertwined!

Mirrors of the Meadow

In mirrors reflecting laughter's grace,
We see the jests painted on our face.
A meadow blooming with comical cheer,
Where daisies whisper jokes for all to hear.

Butterflies giggle, swapping their wings,
As ants in hats perform silly things.
Each blade of grass holds stories untold,
In nature's humor, we marvel bold.

With echoes of laughter bouncing around,
In this meadow's depths, joy's truly found.
We trip over daisies; we tumble and fall,
Yet laughter lifts us, it conquers all.

So let's dance with mirrors, reflect on the fun,
In this silly meadow under the sun.
With every chuckle, our spirits will soar,
In the realm of laughter, there's always more!

Tides of Returning

The ocean waves do laugh and sway,
Like pants on a clown, in play.
They pull back the sand, then tease it near,
Like a dog with a bone, oh dear!

Seagulls cry, with a cheeky squawk,
As they strut around like they own the block.
The fish below roll their eyes in jest,
"We're stuck with these jokers, it's quite the fest!"

The tide slips away with a playful grin,
Only to return and splash us again.
Each wave has a giggle, a splash, a cheer,
"Oh, here comes that ocean, get ready, my dear!"

Life's rhythms shift in a dance of glee,
As we tumble through time, like a wild bumblebee.
With each ebb and flow, we gain a new song,
The ocean's a jester, and we all sing along!

A Dance of New Leaves

Tiny buds peek out, a little shy,
Ballet slippers on trees, oh my!
Branches shimmy, twirl without care,
"Who needs the spring? We'll dance in bare air!"

The wind joins the fun, a cheeky friend,
Whispering jokes as the leaves descend.
"Get your act together! No room for old,
The disco's alive, come on, be bold!"

Blossoms giggle, shake off their sleep,
Spinning in circles, in laughter so deep.
"Don't get stuck in winter and mumble,
Join us in this footloose tumble!"

With each little sway, they catch the sun's rays,
Their brightness ignites those oh-so-fun days.
So waltz with the breeze, as the colors unfold,
In a jolly old dance, forever retold!

A Symphony of Springs

Water droplets tap a lively beat,
Nature's orchestra on every street.
The frogs croak solos from the lily pads,
"Let's kick it up, we're all wild and mad!"

Birds chirp a tune that makes dogs bark,
Squirrels join in, with a feisty spark.
Tunes of life play, no notes to waste,
Join in the revelry, let's have some haste!

Butterflies flutter with jazz hands wide,
Creating a ruckus a stone's throw outside.
Beetles on trumpets, ladybugs hum,
This symphony's sizzling, oh, here they come!

So dance in the rain, or hop on a tune,
Spring's merry concert is over the moon.
Share laughter and joy, sing praises all night,
In this lively uplift, everything feels just right!

Mesmerized by the Past

Old photos giggle from dusty books,
While grandpa tells tales that give us the hooks.
"Remember when I danced with a broom?
It swept me off my feet, what a glamorous doom!"

With gadgets bygone, we laugh and sigh,
Mismatched socks had a heyday, oh my!
From floppy disks to selfies, what a change,
But the stories remain, no matter how strange.

Each wrinkle tells tales of mischief and fun,
Of adventures crafted under the sun.
"Did I really wear that?" we ponder and muse,
"Every style was a hit! Who could we refuse?"

So here's to the past, let's twaddle and weave,
In the fabric of time, what joy we conceive!
With laughter as gold, and memories a blast,
We embrace the antics, mesmerized by the past!

Conduits of Life

In the garden of giggles, the weeds play tricks,
They host wild parties, with sun and with wicks.
Plants wear sunglasses, thinking they're cool,
While daisies dance disco, breaking every rule.

The worms in tuxedos, so classy, so bright,
Debate about sunshine, from morning to night.
Their compost confetti floats high in the air,
As laughter erupts from the roots down, with flair.

In laughter and folly, they find their own way,
Each sprout a comedian, brightening the day.
With every new bud, the punchlines are spun,
Nature's humor is endless; they're having their fun.

So here's to the flowers, the weeds, and the trees,
In this wacky kingdom, they do as they please.
Life's joy unravels in a playful disguise,
Amidst all the chaos, there's wisdom that lies.

The Essential Embrace

In the pub of the forest, where branches all meet,
A hug from a grapevine is truly a treat.
The oak tells a tale, it's quite a tall tale,
While chestnuts throw acorns, to ensure they won't fail.

Apple trees giggle, their fruits in a rush,
As squirrels hold fashion shows, in a stylish hush.
Pine needles whisper, "You're looking quite green,"
While ferns twirl in laughter, and dance on the scene.

With every embrace, they weave stories anew,
In this tangled-up humor, all nature's askew.
The laughter of leaves mixes sweet with the sound,
Of roots high in jests, where joy is unbound.

So gather, dear friends, in this woodland delight,
Where life's silly moments shine brilliant and bright.
The hugs that we share, from the earth up above,
Remind us that humor is part of the love.

When Silence Gives Way

In the still of the night, a frog hops with glee,
Croaking secrets and jokes for the stars to see.
The crickets keep time with their rhythmic ballet,
As moonbeams chuckle, "Let's lighten the sway!"

A leaf rustles softly, with laughter so near,
It whispers a riddle for all willing to hear.
The owls roll their eyes, in a wise, funny manner,
As shadows play tricks on the path of a planner.

When silence gives in, humor starts to weave,
Mysteries lighten, where darkness might grieve.
The trees bend in laughter, their branches a sway,
Reminding us all, it's a whimsical play.

So join in the fun, let your worries take flight,
Dance through the stillness, explore the delight.
In the night's gentle humor, find joy in your day,
When silence gives way, let the laughter hold sway.

Fragments of Foliage

Scattered around, like confetti from trees,
Are leaves redoing their stand-up routines,
In clusters of colors, they share all their quirks,
While branches snicker at the antics of jerks.

The shrubs play charades, acting out their tales,
With petals that flutter, like miniature sails.
A gnarled little willow, proud of its flair,
Cracks jokes with the breeze, as they tumble through air.

Fragments of stories, tucked under the bark,
Eagerly bickering, they push up the dark.
Each shrub has a laugh, at the trees who stand tall,
Daring them to wobble, daring them to fall.

So let's celebrate nature, with chuckles and peels,
As foliage whispers, it shares how it feels.
In this merry chaos, let laughter take flight,
For every small fragment brings joy to our sight.

Where the Old Paths Lead

In a garden, lost in weeds,
I found a shoe from years gone by,
It whispered tales of wobbly deeds,
And left me giggling, oh my my.

A tortoise raced, or so he thought,
With dreams of speed, he'd have a go,
But slippery lettuce, he just fought,
And ended up with quite a show.

The old path's filled with silly sights,
A gnome who wore a hat too big,
He waved and danced on starry nights,
While I just sat there, giggling, fig.

So wander where the wild things roam,
With laughter as your fun-filled guide,
Each twist and turn, a joke's own home,
Where ancient wonders still collide.

A Tangle of Green

In jungles where the grass grows wild,
A coconut decided to roll,
It bumped a meerkat, oh, so riled,
And both of them just lost control.

A parrot squabbled with a frog,
Over whose song was the best ditty,
Home to the woods, oh, what a slog,
With laughter echoing, oh so witty.

The vines entwined around a post,
They threw a party, raved all night,
With squirrels serving acorn toast,
In their leafy, leafy delight.

A tangle of vines and crazy cheer,
A place where giggles grow in streams,
So if you seek a haven near,
Come join the fun within the dreams.

Whispers of the Earth

In the soil, the worm took stock,
Of broccoli's hilarious past,
It laughed at all the garden talk,
While tickling carrots, unsurpassed.

The daisies joined in witty jest,
As ants paraded in a row,
A tree in bloom just could not rest,
For all the laughter's overflow.

With each breeze, the petals swoon,
They twirled and danced in wild delight,
A taffeta of floral tune,
Creating giggles out of sight.

Earth's whispers bring a joyful round,
Where humor sprouts from roots below,
In every crack and crevice found,
A chuckle's bloom begins to grow.

Hues of Resurgence

In springtime's flair, we start anew,
With paintbrushes, we fill the air,
A purple cow with polka dots,
Amidst the colors, laughter's flair.

The flowers giggle in the breeze,
While paint-splattered frogs then leap,
In hues brighter than the seas,
They leap around and make us peep!

A rainbow stretched across the sky,
With sunshine yellow grinning wide,
The hues do dance and wink an eye,
And swirled away with playful pride.

From each petal to grassy floor,
A burst of color and of cheer,
The canvas of our lives explore,
With laughter painted everywhere.

Awakening the Ancients

The ancestors dance in the breeze,
With wooden shoes and stinky cheese.
They giggle and grin, sharing old tales,
Of mishaps and fumbles, and giant snails.

Crickets join in, a band of cheer,
Playing their tunes for all to hear.
A ruckus of laughter fills the night,
As the past winks softly, oh what a sight!

Old trees murmur secrets of fun,
Whispering jokes under the sun.
They've seen it all, the good and the bad,
And jest about moments that make us glad.

So let's dance with the spirits, join in their jest,
Laughter and joy, they know it's the best.
In the garden of time, we're never alone,
With each silly story, our hearts feel at home.

The Touch of the Earth

When I touch the ground, it wiggles a bit,
A tickle from soil, oh isn't that sweet?
But watch out for worms, they're plotting a prank,
With squiggly jokes right by the plank.

The daisies are giggling, they know what's cool,
Making crowns with clovers, it's a plant school.
The earth's sense of humor is quite the delight,
As ants march in line, marching left and right.

The rocks play it tough, posing all day,
While moss crackles softly, saying, "Hey!
I've been here forever, just having some fun,
In this wild play that's never quite done."

So let's tiptoe lightly, and join in the game,
With each silly squish, we'll never be the same.
For the earth has a rhythm, a bounce, a groove,
In this wacky old dance, it's our hearts we'll move.

Sunlit Breath

The sun wakes up with a stretch and a yawn,
Dancing on rooftops, it's a brand new dawn.
Clouds crack up laughing, wearing their fluff,
While puddles reflect, "Enough is enough!"

Butterflies flutter with quirky loose flair,
In polka-dot costumes, they twirl in the air.
"Why not?" they giggle, "Let's paint the sky!
With colors that make every grump seem shy!"

The breeze blows kisses, a playful delight,
Tickling the petals, such a jubilant sight.
"Dance on the pavement!" the flowers declare,
As they shimmy and sway with the sun in the air.

So bask in the laughter, let joy be the guide,
For the warmth of the sun is a whimsical ride.
In this playground of life, let your spirit swoop,
With bright, merry moments, come on and loop!

Threads of Vital Growth

In the fabric of life, there's yarn all around,
With stitches of giggles and ticks of the ground.
A patchwork of colors, both wild and bright,
Sewing memories in the cool morning light.

The spiders spin tales with webs oh so fine,
With glittering beads, their craft divine.
As squirrels plot mischief from branches up high,
While raccoons performance art under the sky.

Weaving new dreams with each silly twist,
In this playful quilt, nothing is missed.
So grab onto laughter, hold tight to its thread,
As we stitch life together, joy's feast to spread.

With every light breeze, let chuckles arise,
In this tapestry of life, there are only surprise.
Let's craft our own quilt with a smile and a song,
In this garden of giggles, let's all sing along!

Reclamation of the Wild

In the jungle where socks often roam,
A raccoon stole my shoe, made it his home.
The bushes start laughing, they're tickled by glee,
Nature's reclaiming what once belonged to me.

The tree trunks are winking, they've seen much worse,
A squirrel in a tutu, rehearsing his verse.
While vines throw a party, they dance on the roof,
Who knew that the wilderness had such a goof?

Old pathways are muddy, and bears think it's cool,
They splash in the puddles, oh what a pool!
The grasses are gossiping, telling their tales,
About the lost hats and the wind's wild gales.

So here in the wild, with a grin and a cheer,
I join in the madness, shedding a tear.
For nature's own comedy is quite the fine art,
In this theater of life, I play my part.

Veins of Vitality

The flowers are crafting a smoothie so bright,
With petals and pollen, what a tasty sight!
Bees buzzing softly, they're chefs in disguise,
Whipping up nectar, oh, what a surprise!

The worms in the soil hold a cooking class,
Teaching the daisies how to look sassy and fast.
With laughter, they wiggle, the roots join the fun,
Who knew underground life could bask in the sun?

Mushrooms wear sunglasses, they strut with such flair,
Claiming they own all the fungi out there.
While ants in a line sing a march to the beat,
Dancing their way to a banquet so sweet!

Life's vibrant connections all tangled in glee,
Nature's own network, buzzing like a bee.
With chuckles and giggles, oh what a delight,
In the veins of the wild, everything feels right!

Cascading Newness

A waterfall giggles as it tumbles down,
Splashing on pebbles, it wears quite a crown.
Fish leap like dancers in a grand fish ballet,
Making waves of laughter at the end of the day.

The sky drops confetti from clouds made of fluff,
While rabbits are thumping their feet—what a ruff!
Each drop brings a joke, a silly surprise,
Life's bubbly antics twinkle in our eyes.

Rivers are racing, they're fit as a fiddle,
While frogs play the banjo, hopping in the middle.
The banks laugh uproariously, shaking with cheer,
As squirrels toss acorns, their party's sincere!

With each little ripple, new joys come to mind,
In the splash of the water, we're all intertwined.
So let's all be merry, let the fresh fun flow,
In the cascade of life, let's steal the whole show!

Dance of the Dandelions

Dandelions waltz in the breeze with such grace,
They twirl in the sunlight, all smiles on their face.
With each little puff, they send seeds on the roam,
A fluffy parade, oh, they call it home!

The lawn's in a tangle, with flowers in fight,
While butterflies giggle and join in the night.
Each petal that dances, spinning round in delight,
Looks back at the gardener, with a wink and a bite.

Grass blades are clapping, they cheer for the show,
While snails pull up front, to enjoy the grand flow.
The daisies are judging, with scores on a leaf,
As dandelions bloom in their bright, bold motif.

And when the sun sets, they gather in crowds,
Making dandelion wishes and dreaming aloud.
In the dance of the wild, there's humor anew,
With every bright bloom, life continues to skew!

In the Cradle of Change

In the land where odd things grow,
A sock-tree sprouts, and off it flows.
Socks dance blissfully in the breeze,
While birds sing tunes of apple cheese.

The ants wear shades, parade in line,
On beetle backs, they sip on wine.
With laughter echoing through the glade,
Change is a game we all have played.

A snail in slippers joins the fest,
Saying, 'Move to slow? Well, that's the best!'
They twirl and whirl, without a care,
In the cradle of fun, we all share.

So if you find a tree of socks,
Join the dance, unbind the locks.
For in this place, with no refrain,
We laugh and change, it's all a game.

Flames of the Hearth

There once was a fire that grew too bold,
It turned the marshmallows to molten gold.
With giggles and snorts, the flames did prance,
And sparked up laughter in a silly dance.

The cat wore shades and bopped to the beat,
While squirrels were twirling, happy on their feet.
The hotdogs serenaded the dancing beans,
Turning moments into cooking scenes.

'This cozy spot,' the raccoon said,
'Is where we gather, and fears are shed.'
With popcorn popping in joyful cheer,
We stoke the flames, spreading good cheer.

Thus laughter roasts as we share a meal,
In flames of warmth, we feel the deal.
With jokes and stories around the way,
Our hearts ignite in this fire play.

The Awakening Grove

In the grove where giggles bloom,
The trees wear hats in a fine costume.
With branches swaying to the jest,
They host a party, a leafy fest.

Squirrels sport suits, so dapper and neat,
While bunnies tap dance on furry feet.
A mushroom clown juggles acorn pies,
As the sun winks with laughter in its eyes.

The twinkling brook joins in the cheer,
Singing silly songs that all can hear.
In this space, joy spreads like dew,
Awakening spirits, both old and new.

So come and join this lively show,
Where even the shadows can't help but glow.
In the awakening, spirits arise,
With whispers of fun under sunny skies.

Beneath the Canopy

Beneath the leaves, a party brews,
Where ants in bowties serve up the news.
The beetles roll dice on a patch of moss,
Playing games without a loss.

A wise old owl gave a wink and nod,
As a little fox danced with a sod.
The chatter of critters filled the air,
Joyously tangled in their own affair.

Pillows of petals scattered around,
They're lounging while giggles abound.
A hedgehog plays the banjo with flair,
While fireflies glow without a care.

So when you wander through forests wild,
Remember it's all just laughter compiled.
In this canopy of fun we find,
The humor of nature, sweetly intertwined.

Tides of Transformation

The waves come crashing, making a fuss,
They dance with the sand, causing a ruckus.
Everyone's running, but can't get away,
It's just Mother Nature, putting on a play.

The tides are tired, a bit out of breath,
They scrunch up their faces, taunting to death.
Who knew the ocean could act so bizarre?
Like a dramatic artist, a real superstar?

Seashells chuckle, caught in the flow,
As seaweed wiggles, putting on a show.
Crabs with their pinchers go comically sideways,
And dolphins pop up, cracking jokes in the waves.

So let's ride the crest with a grin ear to ear,
Embracing each flip, with laughter and cheer.
In this wavy world where silliness sprouts,
Life's oceanic dance is what it's about!

Fresh shoots on Ancient Grounds

In gardens of laughter, where old meets the new,
Tiny green sprouts are working on their debut.
They poke up their heads, like kids with a prank,
"Look at us, we're growing! Give thanks to the dank!"

The worms are all giggling, they squirm with delight,
As old roots reminisce in the soft moonlight.
"Hey, remember when we were spry and so spry?
Now we're just stories, but my, oh my!"

With sunshine as laughter, and rain as a cheer,
These seedlings are bouncing, filled up with good beer.
Dandelions toast to the weeds that they know,
"Mighty fine company, let's put on a show!"

So raise up your glasses to green leaves just spry,
For every old tale is a wink from the sky.
In the dance of existence, some giggles abound,
As fresh shoots erupt on ancient grounds.

The Cycle Unfolds

Round and round we go, like a merry-go-round,
Seasons are comedians, no grumpy old hound.
Winter shivers, throws snowflakes that slip,
While summer laughs loud with a sunburnt quip.

Fall chuckles at leaves, as they twirl through the air,
"Catch me if you can!" they play without a care.
Spring hops in, wearing a crown of bright buds,
Yet naps like a cat on the soft warm muds.

The cycle's a jester, a trickster so bold,
With time as the audience, oh the stories told!
Each twist and each turn, brings fresh comic relief,
The stage is eternal, no room for the grief.

So let's join the jesters in this wacky parade,
For life's just a skit, where we're all meant to jade.
In laughs and in turns, let the fun be our mold,
As we dance with the seasons, each story unfolds.

Beneath the Surface

In puddles of giggles, there's chaos down low,
Fish hold auditions for the funniest show.
"Who's got the best splash?" one tiny fin shouts,
As they flail for the crown among giggly bouts.

Beneath the calm pond lies a ruckus of cheer,
Where frogs are the judges, with warts to appear.
They croak out the scores, keeping rhythm with glee,
Oh, what a strange fable, a sight to see!

Turtles shuffle in, wearing caps oh so bright,
Boasting slow dance moves, they twirl with delight.
"Watch out now, speedy!" they wink from their shell,
In this bubbling madness, the water says, "Well?"

So dive into laughter, there's magic down there,
Life's truly absurd when it's churning with flare.
Each splash is a punchline, a comic confuse,
The surface is rocky, but joy's what we choose!

Guardians of the Green

In the park, the squirrels conspire,
Plotting acorn heists, they never tire.
A rabbit hops in, all sassy and bold,
Claiming that he found treasure of old.

They play a game of hide and seek,
With laughing leaves, causing quite a squeak.
Each tree is a castle, each branch a throne,
In the court of nature, they're never alone.

Lush Paths Forward

Follow the trail where daisies shout,
A worm in a hat twirls round about.
The grass tickles toes, as they dance and sway,
Bouncing beholders, come join the play!

A bear in a tutu, twirls with delight,
As bees in top hats buzz through the night.
The path is paved with giggles and cheer,
Who knew the wilds could be so dear?

Blossoms of Forgotten Dreams

In a garden of socks, flowers sprout,
Where old dreams bloom, you just can't doubt.
They whisper secrets, tales of the old,
Like a mischievous cat with yarn made of gold.

Each petal's a laugh, each stem a fun poke,
As the wind tells jokes, and the sun just boke.
Even the weeds are wild and gay,
Reveling in sunshine, come what may.

The Cycle of Becoming

Caterpillars sip tea with grace,
Discussing the merits of a new face.
With tiny top hats, they plot their delight,
Transforming into butterflies, ready for flight.

The ladybugs munch on leaves of fate,
Playing chess with ants, it's never too late.
As the sun sets low, they cheer for the night,
In the whimsical world, everything's right.

Nature's Comeback

In the garden, weeds do dance,
Chasing bugs, they take a chance.
Sunflowers giggle in the breeze,
While daisies hang from the trees.

The branches stretch, a funny sight,
As squirrels play tag, oh what a fright!
The ants march in their little lines,
Wearing hats made out of twines.

The rain clouds drip like leaky taps,
While frogs perform their silly flaps.
Nature laughs, a cheerful ace,
In a wild and wacky race!

Amidst the chaos, life prevails,
With blooming jokes it never fails.
The earth high-fives with roots so sly,
And tickles the sky, oh my, oh my!

From Dust to Bloom

From dusty ground to flowered glee,
A cactus wore a cup of tea.
And lettuce laughed in leafy cheer,
While broccoli picked up a beer.

A little bud, with giggles bright,
Claimed it grew overnight!
With petals painted like a clown,
It danced around, it twirled down.

The mulch threw a party, oh so grand,
Where worms brought their band to the land.
Lettuce and radishes formed a line,
Shaking their roots, feeling divine!

From soil's embrace, a raucous spree,
Where laughter thunders, wild and free.
With a whisper, the flowers croon,
Life's a jest that ends too soon.

The Unseen Revival

Beneath the soil, a ruckus brews,
While moles wear ties and sing the blues.
There's rumbles, giggles, 'neath the ground,
As mushrooms pop up all around!

With roots that tickle and twist with flair,
The carrots decide they want to share.
Potatoes joke, 'We're underground!
We hold the best, the funniest ground!'

The rains have come, with splashes bold,
So every sprout feels brave and bold.
Earthworms slide, a twisting fun,
In a parade that has just begun!

From the dark depths of muddy beds,
To the light above, where laughter spreads.
The unseen forces weave their play,
As life refreshes, come what may!

Between Seasons

In the space where seasons mix,
The trees tell jokes; their bark does tricks.
Autumn's leaves in a twirled fight,
With summer's sun—oh what a sight!

Winter grumbles with frosty breath,
While spring plants joke, 'Ain't life a fest?'
The critters gather, a motley crew,
To swap their tales, and sip the dew.

A tulip dons a winter hat,
Says to the snow, 'How do you like that?'
While daffodils giggle in the cold,
And laugh at the stories the squirrels told.

In this quirky in-between,
Life's a comedy, quite the scene!
With every leaf and every breeze,
It's nature's chuckle, a life of ease!

www.ingramcontent.com/pod-product-compliance
Lightning Source LLC
Chambersburg PA
CBHW071815160426
43209CB00003B/102

9781805670049